Frazzled Heart

Ashish Gupta

ISBN 978-93-5458-342-1
© Ashish Gupta 2021
Published in India 2021 by Pencil

A brand of
One Point Six Technologies Pvt. Ltd.
123, Building J2, Shram Seva Premises,
Wadala Truck Terminal, Wadala (E)
Mumbai 400037, Maharashtra, INDIA
E connect@thepencilapp.com
W www.thepencilapp.com

Author biography

Ashish Gupta grew up in Faridabad, a town near Delh where his father worked as an engineer at a thermal power plant. Initially focusing on science, Ashish did his Bachelor of Science and Post Graduation in Management .

After spending most of his initial years in marketing line, he quit his job and planned to pursue his passion, that of writing stories.

Starting with short stories, Frizzled Heart is his first attempt at writing a novel.

CONTENTS

Cute Girl

This is the story of a lovely young girl who possessed one of most the beautiful faces I had ever seen. Every single line on her face was carefully chiseled; a living testimony to God's craftsmanship. Her dimpled cheeks added to her beauty and were a delight to watch when she smiled. Her hairs were shiny black, hanging artfully down her back to form a ponytail. As if to complete her facial beauty, God endowed her with a pair of deep grey eyes full of pristine innocence and honesty.

Not only was she beautiful from outside, she was blessed with a most beautiful heart as well, always full of love for others. She could motivate people to bring the best out of them. She had the ability to make dead men laugh. She could joke without offence and wink an eye to express what she dare not utter. She made anyone want to be a better person.

Suffice it to say, she had that indomitable spirit of a winner, who could charm the hearts of her adversaries by her innocence and childish pranks.

I had not seen someone so beautiful, both from outside as well as inside.

A year ago I did not even know she existed. I had my first

encounter with her during the last year of my school. She was one class behind me. One day, during our lunch break, while I and my friend were having lunch in the gallery facing our classroom, I had an eerie feeling of a pair of eyes staring on my back. Upon turning, we saw a pretty girl staring at me and smiling truantly. Her queer behaviour made me feel very awkward. With bewildered face, I confronted the girl and asked the reason for her strange behavior. To my amazement, she did not utter a single word but kept on smiling softly, making me feel even more nervous. Soon nervousness turned into anger which was beginning to spiral out of control. She did not seem to bother, standing still as if nothing had happened. All through the commotion, my friend had remained a silent spectator. When I could not hold it any longer, grinding my teeth, I repeated my question, this time with a certain amount of force, to show her my intent of getting an answer. To my amazement she kept mum and continued smiling. Now my anger coupled with amazement and frustration knew no bounds. I did not have a clue as what she was up to.

Mentally I was trying to figure out the puzzle, when I was startled by sound of the bell that signaled the end of the lunch break and I had to move back to my class with the unanswered questions weighing heavily on my mind. I resolved to get answers to those questions at the first available opportunity. But that menacing girl denied me that opportunity even. She had her own plans. No sooner had the class ended; I saw her standing outside, waiting for me. Her face bore an expression of extreme remorse which made me forget my anger instantly. Instead, I became worried for her. It looked as if she had been fighting with herself for long. Upon setting her eyes on me, she reached for me immediately and before I could think of anything, she started on her own as if she had been rehearsing her response and wanted to bare it all in one single breath.

According to her account, she had placed a bet with her friend, the idea being to irritate me to the point that I get mad at her and pluck my hairs in desperation. Now that simple explanation of her strange behavior raised another question in my inquisitive mind and I confronted her with that.
Out of all the other students in the school, why did she choose me as the subject of her prank?

Pat came her reply, I possessed one of the most innocent faces she had ever come across, making me a perfect subject for her bet. Her candid response made me blush. I did not know how to react to her revelation: whether to take it positively and laugh it off or feel angry about it. Nonplussed, I stood still, with bewildered eyes.

Reading my mind and blaming her for my predicament, she began to sob silently and gestured for my forgiveness. Her pretty, ever smiling face was all drenched in tears. It was not difficult to understand that she was sincerely sorry for her act and sought my pardon.

I stood still, staring at her for a few moments, trying to decide on my reaction, when a gentle smile escaped my face. Sensing victory, a sigh of relief relaxed her tense muscles and she broke into a convulsive laughter, making me laugh with her as well. For the next few minutes we just stood there, staring at each other and laughing carelessly, oblivious to the fact that we were still in the school.

We might have continued with our stupid act had not the vice principal of our school passed by and seen us. Her immediate reaction was a slight grin, but she controlled her emotions perfectly. Her responsibility as a person of authority did not allow such a reaction. She motioned us to follow her towards her office.

Five minutes later we were seated at the table opposite her. Without wasting any time, our vice principal came to the point directly and asked us the reason for our strange behavior in a stern voice. Her eyes darted quickly from one face to another without a flutter, looking inquiringly into our eyes for some honest answers. Nervousness due to lack of any reasonable explanation sealed our lips. She allowed us a few minutes to calm our racing nerves and respond. When both of us remained silent even after that, her temper flared and she made us count the number of school rules we had broken in those few minutes making us perfect cases for severe punishment.

Finding ourselves in a hopeless situation, I opened my mouth to respond but the girl gestured me to keep shut. She took it upon herself to answer the vice principal. She laid the account of the happenings of the morning before her in their due order and apologized for her irresponsible behavior. She took the whole blame on her shoulders and pleaded with the vice principal to let me go unpunished.

Her honest response struck the right cords with the vice principal. She sat for a moment in complete silence, tapping her chin with a pencil, trying to make up her mind about the current situation.

After few agonizing minutes of pindrop silence, she asked the girl for her school details, which the latter eagerly supplied. The vice principal checked those details with the school records. Her hard expressions relaxed immediately. The records confirmed the girl in question to be a meritorious student of her class and daughter of one of the highly rated trustees of the school. Without any further questioning she let us off with a warning- next time repetition would mean a severe punishment.

We came out of the vice principal's office a little red faced but surely enjoying every bit of the little encounter with her. In fact, that incident has been etched as one of the most cherished memories of my childhood days. Even today it brings a glitter of smile when my thoughts wander to that particular day.

That was the first time, ever since our brief exchange that I came to know about her.

Her name was Shobha. She belonged to a highly affluent Anglo-Indian family. Her father was a known businessman of the area, owner of a big engineering company. Though his business interests took him all over the world yet he was always happy to be back in his country. He remained attached to his roots. He was a very pious man, known for his generosity. Humility, hard work, benevolence, and punctuality were his key qualities. He was also one of the main trusties of our school. Her mother was of Canadian descent. Shobha was their only child and so raised in affluence. She led a pampered life. Even her tiniest wish never went unfulfilled. A battery of attendants was always available at her disposal. She moved about the city in the most expensive of the cars and played with expensive toys, much to the envy of other children around her. She had never experienced the feeling associated with tears falling from one's eyes.

In fact it would not be an understatement to say that life had been more than generous to her- loving parents, a big house replete with luxuries, eye catching beauty accompanied by heart winning manners. She had it all that one could wish for.

Her types of comforts were enough to spoil anyone but Shobha. Her feet always remained firmly rooted to the ground, like her father. She was far above arrogance. Though she might have inherited the beauty of her mother; she had the heart of her father.

After the school was over, we spent close an hour recollecting the events of the day and laughing our hearts out.

At that time we were totally unaware that life was taking a slow curious turn for both of us which would become evident in the days to come.

Each passing day brought us closer and we started to enjoy each other's company.

I started to steal some extra minutes from busy morning hours to get ready for the school, taking good care of my personal details, glancing at the mirror numerous times. It had never been part of my habbit to look into the mirror more than once but there I was looking at it multiple times. My parents found it strange initially, as I had always been indifferent to my physical appearances, but gradually they dismissed it as another teenage craze.

At the breakfast table, I found myself in hurry to finish my food, taking two gulps at a time, often ignoring my mother's advice to go slow. Thereafter I would paddle my way to the school as hard as I could just to reach there early and meet Shobha. Ditto was with her. She too found it hard to spend her time at home and remained eager to rush to the school. Her parents also felt anxious about the sudden change in her behaviour but she calmed them with a gentle smile. They had full faith in the upbringing of their daughter and there was no reason for them to distrust her.

It was always a competition as to who would arrive at the school first. Sometimes I was the winner while at the others she came out with flying colours.

Once at the school, we looked to find excuses to meet each other during school hours. Things came to a point where we were prepared to take extra risk just to be in each other's company. Bunking classes was one of those, often enduring tough punishments. Our entire lunch break was spent idling together, paving way to unhealthy gossips. Day at the school ended for us only after we had waived each other goodbye, promising to meet the coming day.

Evenings at home were no different. Unable to think about anything else except Shobha, my feet would automatically take me to her house. I would paddle close to ten kilometers every day to meet her, where she would be eagerly waiting for my arrival. I felt overjoyed just to be standing in front of her house. It was always nice to see her.

Fire of desire to see each other kindled on both sides. It provided us the reason to sing, to cry and above all else, it made us live.

Upon reaching her house, we quickly moved to the confines of her room and spent the whole evening together, talking about anything we could think of; the most common topic of conversation being the events of the day at school. We enjoyed mimicking our teachers and picking out the mistakes of our fellow classmates. Shobha had the habbit of talking rapidly and animatedly. Her way of recital made the topic even more exciting. Frankly, I was not so much interested in the conversation as I was in the way she talked. I liked sitting besides her watching her talk, inhaling deeply the sweet smell of her body perfume, watching her pretty face moving perfectly while she talked and often curl into a lovely dimpled smile. For me it was a worthy sight. Her proximity brought me an altogether different type of happiness the kind of which I had never felt before. There was something special about her.

The routine was diligently followed almost every single day. Any break from that set pattern was unacceptable to her. It was greeted with angry telephone inquiries and a difficult time at school the following day. She would be freaking mad and would ignore me the whole day. It would take some herculean efforts to cheer up her mood.

My frequent visit to Shobha's house provided her parents an opportunity to know me better and soon they developed a liking for me too. They never objected to our friendship, but made sure we did not cross our limits. I had few chances of meeting Shobha's father as he generally remained out of town but her mother took good care of us both. She kept us amply stocked supplies of a variety of homemade snacks and loved watching us enjoy her preparations. Her home baked cake was a specialty and my favourite. She loved preparing it for me whenever I requested for it.

Every evening at her house was a splendid, exciting evening and we would always part with a heavy heart.

Our closeness kept us so involved with each other that we started to drift away from our other friends. One day my best befriend, Rohan, requested me to help him solve a mathematics problem but I was so busy with Shobha that I shrugged him off, creating a never ending rift between us. That was just one such incident. Instances like that started to happen almost daily. Our friends started to ignore us but we did not seem to bother.

Within no time, words about our closeness spread like wild fire throughout the school and soon became the talk of everybody's lips.

Finding two of their best students getting emotionally involved and neglecting their studies, the teachers decided to discuss the matter with the Principal. The reputation of the school and our future lives were at stake.

It was the first such incident of its kind that had ever happened in the school history. Moreover, it involved the daughter of one of its main trustees and the school management did not want it to blow out of proportion. So they instructed the Principal to handle it with extra care and exercise maximum restraint.

We were summoned to the Principal's office. Once there, we were apprised of the situation that our relationship was creating and how harmful it was becoming for the school environment as well as for our future lives. According to our teachers, getting into a relationship was only human and natural. There was nothing wrong about it but it should be entered into at its proper time. There is a proper time for everything in life. Currently our time required us to study hard to do well in the examinations and get admissions in reputed institutions. Wasting our time in a frivolous manner like that was only going to ruin our future instead of doing it any good.

More such concerns were raised. Every teacher had her own suggestion to make. Each seemed to press upon her point more than the others but their suggestions lacked conviction. It was like as if they were trying to impress the Principal.

The counseling session went on for almost an hour and we sat there like two obedient kids, nodding our heads in agreement on the outside but laughing inside. Once or twice we even exchanged mischievous glances which could not escape the eyes of our teachers.

Finding their advice falling on deaf ears made the Principal and the teachers angry. At last, feeling frustrated and tired of their wasted efforts, it was decided to call our parents.

As planned, the situation was discussed in front of our parents the next day. Naturally they were very livid and wanted the school to take strict disciplinary action against us. But keeping in mind the best of our interests and the interests of the school, it was decided to separate us for our own good. Since it was my last year in the school, I was told to prepare for my upcoming board examinations from my home and to come to school only when absolutely necessary, while Shobha was to remain in school and continue with her studies.

And that's how we two were separated and I saw the last of her.....

Breakup

I started to prepare for the examinations from my home. But I found it difficult to concentrate. The moment I opened my book, Shobha's innocent, beautiful face smiled at me and I was lost in her thoughts. Each textbook word seemed to resemble her face. I missed her deeply and felt lonely. Her thoughts tormented me, making me sad. Sometimes I even wept in silence.

In those testing times, my parents became my best friends. They made sure to spend more and more of their precious time with me whenever I felt lonely and depressed. My mother took extra care of me when my father was off to office. She came to my study every few minutes and kept me well supplied with refreshments. She caressed my hairs lovingly while I was busy concentrating on my studies. She often took my head in her lap and massaged in a bid to refresh my tired mind, in spite of my protestations. My father checked my progress in my studies regularly and made sure I was carrying on fine. He was always there to take care of any doubts.

It was then that I realized that parents are a child's best friend and will always be there for him.

With the passage of time and the pressure of upcoming

board examinations memories of Shobha soon started to fade. Timely guidance from my parents also played a big role. I was once again whole heartdly absorbed in preparing for my upcoming examinations, the date for which had finally been announced.

I wrote my board examinations with full confidence and preparation and true to my expectations I passed them with flying colours. To double up my success, I also secured admission to one of the top colleges of the country.

My happiness knew no bounds and I wanted to share it with everyone, especially Shobha. My parents granted me permission to contact her without any hesitation. I was going to contact her after many months, the very thought of which made my heart flutter. With shaking hands I dialed her phone number and waited with baited breath for it to be answered, but to my utter disappointment, the phone stood disconnected. I visited her house that evening but found it occupied by some other family. Upon inquiry, I was told that the earlier landlords had sold them the house and left for an undisclosed destination.

Unable to contact Shobha and share my happiness with her left me shattered once again. Her memories began to haunt me. Her gentle, innocuous smile started to torment my heart and I started to sob silently. Alert to the situation, my mother quickly took over. She announced a grand party to celebrate my success. Rest of the day was spent planning the event.

The party turned out to be a grand success, attended by all

the near and dear ones. I was surrounded by most of my school mates. All were there except Shobha. My eyes were contantly searching for her in the hope that somehow she might have got the news of the party from someone and would come, but that was not to be. As the party progressed, the remotest chance of Shobha turning up also vanished. The realization, of her not coming any more, made me sad but soon I settled down and started to enjoy the evening with my friends and relatives. Thoughts of Shobha never came back again that day.

From that day on I just had few fleeting thoughts of Shobha. I started to get more and more absorbed with my daily routine and my parents made sure to keep me busy. As the day to join college drew near, most of my time was spent giving final touches to my preparations. I started to look forward to the college life.

New start

The day I started for my college, all my school friends and their memories were left behind. The very thought of going into a totally new environment and making new friends filled my heart with certain strange excitement which was beyond description. It was the beginning of a new life welcoming me into its fold with open arms, which I grabbed immediately without any second thoughts.

Life at college was too hectic but exciting. Soon I found myself busy in college life. Joining a good educational institution has its own virtues and vices. If we were sure of a successful future, the arduous lecture sessions and countless home assignments left us with very little time to think of anything else. Weekends were the only days that were left to us to take care of our personal needs and sometimes they too were also used up in completing subject assignments.

The in between semester breaks were spent resting our tired minds at home with least bit of inclination to go elsewhere. Once or twice I tried to trace Shobha, during the breaks, but could not get any leads to her whereabouts. If rumors were to be believed her family had left the town for good after her schooling. With many efforts I was able to get hold of the school records and scanned them for her information but there too I came out blank. The only information that I could lay my hands on was her passing the board exams with flying colours making the school proud of her performance. I gave a silent ovation to her outstanding achievement and left the school.

Time flew quickly as if it had wings, days slipped into weeks, weeks turned into months and months transformed into years and soon I was staring at the end of our college life. Companies were holding campus interviews and I was one of the few lucky ones to be picked up by a reputed company offering me a handsome remuneration package. The offer was good in every respect except the posting was to be in a city far off from my home which would take me away from my parents. I would have to leave my parents and settle in some unknown land.

Since it was my first job and the start of my professional career, I took the offer with a great deal of excitement. The prospect of moving away from my parents did bother me but not much, as I had got accustomed to solitary living since my college days. My parents also seemed extremely excited and supported me, as always. Whatever pain they felt did not show on their humble faces; they hid it behind their parental smiles.

I became busy preparing for my upcoming professional life after my return from the college. Moreover, I wanted to spend maximum amount of time with my parents, unsure of when I would be able to see them once I join the office.

Finally the day drew close to start my professional life. I

left my home with a heavy heart. Farewell at the station was equally emotional. Tears filled the eyes of all of us. I could feel a lump form in my throat, making it hard to speak. The condition of my parents was no different. But they were parents and not supposed to show their emotional weakness, lest it might come in the way of their child's progress. They took the parting very bravely and kept on waving at me till the train had gone out of sight.

Once the parting was over and after the train had picked up speed leaving my parents far behind, I steadied my somber mood, made myself comfortable and closed my eyes, picturing my life ahead.

I reached my destination a day earlier. An office cab had been sent to pick me up. Soon I was moving towards the officer's hostel where a room had been allotted to me as a temporary arrangement. The route to the hostel was breath taking. The road was bouncy but clean. Grass and wild flowers dotted the area. I could see hills at a distance, covered with greenery. The air was chilly and fresh prompting me to take a deep lungful of it.

The hostel was situated in one of the most picturesque surroundings I had ever seen. The building itself was an architectural marvel. Upon reaching the hostel, I was shown to my room. It was a neatly kept room with ample space and equipped with all the necessities. The solitary window to my room opened on the back side of the hostel and presented me a clear view of the hills beyond. The area was lush with mountain trees. Clean and fresh mountain air flowed through the window, sweeping all my laziness away. I spent the rest of the day unpacking my things and setting them neatly at their proper places in the room. In the evening, after the tea, I went outside and took a stroll around the area. The day culminated with a nice dinner and early sleep.

Joining the office went off smoothly the next day. I reached half an hour early and waited at the office reception. At the appointed time, my manager met me and greeted me to the new office. He took me around, introducing me to my seniors and colleagues, who were going to be part of my team. Pleasantries exchanged, I was deputed to an assistant manager who handed me a detailed job description.

The day passed off rapidly. There was so much to absorb that morning. My immediate senior was a jovial man of pleasing personality and amiable manners. He took me through the various procedures without a single frown. He explained each process patiently in a fatherly manner as if I was his child instead of his junior. As for me, I tried to absorb as much as I could without showing any sign of fatigue or disinterest. I hardly had a moment to myself to think about anything but work. I couldn't believe how quickly the day was gone.

No sooner had my boss signaled me the end of the day and time for me to leave, I gathered my jacket, picketed up my bag, wished him goodbye and hurried for my hostel. The first thing I did on reaching my room was to call my parents and describe my first day at office. They were very happy to hear my excited voice and gave me a patient hearing.

After talking to them for some minutes, I loosened up, freshened myself and went for my evening tea. Tea was always served in the common mess and a lively event. Office returners came in groups to savour the rich aroma of evening tea chatting boisterously. Since I was new to that environment and had not befriended anyone till then, I mainly remained to myself.

Once I had finished my tea, I had nothing else to do except to sit idle in my room and watch television or lie down on my bed and relax. I had no mood to do both. So I took that opportunity to check the nearby area. I scurried through the city the whole evening and came back around dinner time. A cursory look at the city impressed me. It was a nice place to dwell into.
Dinner was served at exactly 8.30 pm after which I went for an early rest, all tired up on my first day at the office.

I woke up early the next day and after going through my daily routines, went out for a morning walk towards the small jungle behind my hostel. It was a densely wooded area. The air was fresh and invigorating; in contrast to the big cities. Sweet smell of wild flowers filled the air. The cool rays of rising Sun, falling on crystal clear waters of a mountain lake turning it golden yellow was a sight to behold; the melodious chirping of jungle birds, sitting on tree tops added poetry to the serene environment. I tried to inhale as much of the fresh air as I possibly could and filled my interiors, with morning freshness, to the brim. I was lost to the view-staring, trying to absorb the beauty.

Since I had some spare minutes, I thought of utilizing them watching nature at its very best. I chose a comfortable spot beneath a tree by the lake and sat there looking at the clear still waters changing its colours as the Sun's rays grew in their intensity.

After spending my spare time inhaling deeply the wonders of Mother Nature, I retraced my steps to the hostel and prepared myself for another day at the office.

I got so enamoured by the sight in the jungle that I followed the above routine almost daily, spending my entire spare time watching and trying to figure out the mysteries of nature.

Mysterious girl

It was on one such visit to the lake that I caught sight of a sleek brown body, clad in tatters and holding a forlorn demeanour; peering at me from behind a tree. Something about her caught my attention. I rose from my sitting position and started to step towards her. Sensing my approach she immediately regained her posture and sped away into the jungle; leaving me puzzled.

My mind was brimming with questions. Unable to enjoy the quiet moments any further, I retraced my steps back to my hostel. Throughout the return journey, my mind kept on thinking about that poor lady. Her face kept on reminding me of someone long lost. What intrigued me most was her close resemblance to Shobha. But how could that be possible? On one hand was Shobha, a chirpy city girl from an affluent family, full of life and far away from poverty, while on the other there was that uneducated local hill woman who, it seemed, had never enjoyed city life. Her upkeep clearly spoke of abject poverty.

My condition at the office was no better. With a lot of things running through my mind, it kept on drifting towards the events of the morning. I was unable to concentrate on my work, which did not go unnoticed. Sensing some trouble, my manager enquired me about my confused behaviour, to which I just answered in negative. He seemed unsatisfied with the response but thought it best to keep the matter aside. He advised me to take a few minutes off, compose myself and then return, which I did; but that too did not help much to soothe my tense nerves. My mind still remained foggy. How hard I might try, I was unable to shake my mind off that face in the jungle.

Finally a pathetic day at office came to an end. I came out of the building feeling all confused and carrying a heavy load on my head. Upon reaching the hostel, I went straight for the room. Without bothering to change, I dropped down on the bed, my head throbbing with pain. I tried to soothe down the aching nerves with a cup of evening tea but the clamour at the mess felt unbearable. I returned to my room immediately after only one or two sips and turned on the television so there was a noise to fill the vacuum and provide some semblance of company, but I did not listen or watch. That too I had to switch off immediately as I was unable to stand its sound. I felt nothing but the pain. I skipped dinner as well and went for an early sleep. But that too eluded me. The whole night I kept shifting sides, eagerly waiting for daybreak, when I would try to find answers to my predicament.
No sooner it was light outside; I rushed to the lake in the hope of meeting that woman again. Not finding her at the spot I had seen her the previous morning, I searched every inch of the nearby woods for any sign of her; but in vain. I spent close to an hour in the jungle before returning empty handed.

I felt dejected and weak; inclination to attend office that

day went missing, but since I had just joined the company I could not take the liberty of giving the office a skip so soon. With a pallid face I went to the office. Setting his sights on my condition and taking me to be sick my manager gratefully allowed me a day off.

I went straight to my room and lay down, staring at the empty walls. I do not remember for how long had I slept for when my eyes opened it was dark outside. A quick glance at the watch showed me it was late in the evening. Sleep had provided my tired mind some much needed rest and my head felt better. But that relief proved temporary. My mind soon wandered towards that form in the jungle. The more I thought of it, the more my mind ached from the efforts being put by it. When it became impossible to concentrate any further, I tried to stop thinking and helped myself to a cup of coffee; the warmth of which provided my tense nerves some relief.

I briefly tried many other ideas to relax my mind but it always wandered towards the lady in the jungle. Being new to the place and with no one else to talk to, I found it impossible to share my feeling with someone. It was just me and my disturbing thoughts. I had to take care of them all by myself. But how, I did not know. A feeling of helplessness started to creep upon me and I had a pressing urge to cry myself out.

As normally happens in such situations, finding myself cornered from all sides provided me a new sense of courage. No sooner had the reality dawned on me, my resolve to unravel the mystery grew stronger. I planned to go back to the jungle first thing the next morning and scout for any clues that could lead to that lady. I ate an early dinner and went for the bed. Though sleep was hard to come by, yet I was able to find one and passed my night peacefully.

I borrowed a bike from one of my hostel colleagues next morning, who I had befriended a little and went back to the jungle. Once there, I scanned the area with great care. I went to nearby villages and questioned the locals, providing them with a complete description of the lady I was looking for. They listened to my story with great attention but their blank faces conveyed their answers. Dejected, I returned back.

Not feeling myself in the right frame of mind to carry on my duties, I applied for a few days leave which was promptly sanctioned.

I spent those days scouting the jungle for that mystery woman. I started early and spend the whole day looking for her. I sat besides the lake for hours in the slim hope of seeing the lady, fighting an ever growing sense of dejection; but lady luck did not seem to smile on me. There was no trace of her, as if she had vanished in thin air. Every effort to find her went down the drain.

As days passed by, the chances to find that mysterious lady began to diminish. With each passing day my anxiousness also ebbed. I started to settle down in my daily life and take interest in various other activities apart from finding her.

Needing to breathe a different kind of air, I altered my morning schedule. I stopped visits to the lake; instead I spent those hours going to a gym in the local market. I kept myself busy at the office too; taking keen interest in my routine work and involving myself deeply in each official task, thereby earning the praise of my seniors and colleagues. Within a matter of few days, there was not a single task that I could not perform independently. In a short span of time I became the blue eyed baby of my department.

Memories of the lady had now become a thing of the past. I moved on in life.

Soon, I was looking at the end of a most satisfying first year at my new job. According to company tradition, I received a congratulatory letter from my department head followed by a box of sweets, which was duly shared amongst my team members, with a bouquet of flowers. I felt like the most important person that day.

To make the evening even more memorable, my colleagues arranged a party at a local restaurant known for its incredible interiors and exquisite cuisines. The soft music and candlelight gave it a romantic ambience.

The party went on till late in the evening. It was a most enjoyable, fun filled evening that I could ever remember, which eventually culminated with my manager, who had been my mentor all through that year, heaping accolades on me. Those accolades tasted better than sweets as they had been earned by honesty, hard work and ethical means. I had learned so much being there. My eyes were filled with tears of gratitude.

After quite an evening, as I headed towards my car, I heard my name being called. Perplexed, I spun around and found myself facing the mysterious lady. How could I have missed that voice that had been etched in my heart for the last so many years? I gazed up as in trance. There she was, standing just behind me. I was stunned, unable to move. Words failed me; I did not know what to say or how to react to the situation. I could not believe that she was back the way she was gone from my life.

We continued to stare at each other as if held back by some invisible force; trying to read the other's mind. But all we found was foggy emptiness. The impact of the situation was so intense that we both stood motionless for a long time without uttering a word.

Since it was getting late in the evening and cold was setting in, I suggested her to go to my place. I pulled out my leather jacket and wrapped it around her shoulders and opened the door to the passenger seat of my car motioning her to take the seat. She hesitated for a second and moved in. All through the distance we could not muster the courage to open our mouths and kept silent. There was so much to say but words failed us.

Upon reaching the hostel, I took her to my room and switched on the room lights. The room turned milky white and in its brightness I had a good look at Shobha. Her sight devastated me. As if to look her over better, I brushed back a few stray locks of dark unkempt hair. Her appearance was scruffy and ill kempt. She had been reduced to just a skeleton of her earlier self. Her once beautiful face was pale and etched with sorrow. Her cheeks had gone hollow. There were signs of cuts and bruises all over her skin. She smelled foul and thick layer of dirt covered her skin. She looked in an urgent need of shower. Her sparkling grey eyes had lost their radiance. She was clothed in rags, barely enough to hide her femininity. She presented a sight of complete piteousness and bore a blank expression.

I wrapped my arms around her waist and hugged her tightly, tears rolling down my cheeks. After standing in that position for a few minutes, I separated myself from her. It looked as if she had not fed herself properly for a long time. I took some food out of the refrigerator, warmed it and offered it to her. She grabbed the plate and ate the food hurriedly. Her condition shook me to the heart, I wept from inside. Finally she pushed her plate away, replete for the first time since ages. Once she was done with eating, I prepared coffee for both of us, as, I knew, she was fond of coffee. She accepted the coffee mug with gratitude. I could see traces of tears falling from her eyes.

By the time she finished her coffee it was late in the night. Though I badly wanted her to stay, she had to leave. Staying at the hostel with her would be against social conventions. She wished to go by herself but I forced her to change her mind. I insisted on giving her a lift in my car.

That way I could have some few more minutes to enjoy her company. I had one more solid reason in going with her. I wanted to see her place of dwelling. I had lost her once and I did not want to lose her again. I wanted to be sure that in case she turns her back on me again, where to go looking for her. As if sensing my thoughts, she gave a tired smile and allowed me to accompany her.

All through the ride back to her village she sat tightly besides me, with her head leaned on my shoulder and her eyes closed. She wanted to savour every bit of the moment.She had finally found someone whom she could trust. She felt secure in my company.

Not to mention, I was on cloud nine. I could not believe my luck; I was sitting next to my childhood craze that I had lost once with no hope of finding. I started to hum an old movie song. Hearing me sing she opened her eyes for a quick second and closed them again; a truant smile escaping her pretty lips. I wanted that journey to last forever, savouring the moment for as long as I could.

Finally we reached the destination and it was time for her to depart. She clung to my hand for quite a long time as if unwilling to go. My situation was no better. I wanted to hold on to that hand for eternity. Finally, she pulled her hand and dashed for her house, which was in one of the few huts that were located in front of me. I had so much wished to escort her to her hut but sensing disapproval in her eyes and respecting her privacy, I decided against it. Before leaving I promised to pick her up the next day after office.

Next day at office was one of the most difficult days of my life. For the first time, since I had joined office, time seemed suspended. How much I might have wished for the day to be over, time dragged at its own lazy pace. Every now and then my eyes would automatically move towards the clock to check the time; so uncharacteristic of me. Each time as I glanced at a file or looked for something on the computer, Shobha's smiling face came in front of me. I found myself unable to concentrate on my work. I tried to answer the mails, but could not understand a word of it. Innumerable times I asked for a glass of water or a cup of tea. I even skipped my lunch. My mind seemed to wander somewhere else.

My queer behaviour did not go unnoticed. Sensing something amiss, my manager called me to his cabin and inquired about my well being. I had to assure him with all my conviction that everything was under control. He seemed unconvinced but did not say anything as usual. Somehow the day came to an end.

Finally the clock signaled the end of the day, I collected my things and rushed out; not even glancing back to check the reaction of my colleagues. I was going to meet her. Once on the road my car picked up speed. I was eager to reach Shobha as early as possible.

I found her standing outside her hut, waiting for me. She came running to me the moment she saw my car and hugged me tightly. We stood there in that position for sometime before I motioned her to take her seat in the car.

Colour returns to life

I drove her to the city and took her to the best women's store. There I bought her some new clothes and other woman accessories, much to the astonishment of the curious eyes of the store staff. She looked nothing more than a beggar to them.

Shobha donned her new outfits at the first available opportunity and threw her tatters into a dustbin immediately. She was happy to get rid of them as they reminded her of her recent hardships.

Thereafter, we walked into to a small restaurant. The waiter led us to a table for two in a small corner. I ordered some food for us. The change in environment did a lot of good to Shobha. It proved instrumental in providing her a lot of relief from her treacherous life. She felt elated and within no time she was back to her old self, recounting the little escapades during our school days. Our first encounter was still fresh in her memories. I saw colour return to her lifeless face. She enquired about my last few years and how I landed in that city.

I answered all her queries .Yet whenever I tried to turn the conversation to her traumatic past, she became silent and her eyes went blank, as if requesting me not to take her back to her painful days. Freshness started to drain out of her cheeks again. Taking the cue, I let my curiosity rest till the time she was comfortable enough to relate her past life by herself.

Wanting to spend some more time together we moved towards the loneliness of the woods, where we sat quietly hand in hand, savouring the moment and enjoying each other's company, like we used to do as children at Shobha's house. We only parted when it got very dark and it was time to go.

I could not bear to see her going back to her usual place of dwelling so I booked her a room at a hotel as a temporary stay till the time I find her a proper accommodation. With a heavy heart, I dropped her at the hotel and waving her a good bye I left for my hostel.

Next few days were spent in finding her a proper accommodation. Finally I was able to get one at a reasonable rent. She was initially hesitant to move to her new home. According to her she was already knee deep into my debts and did not want to trouble me any further. Paying her rent meant an extra financial burden on me. But seeing my resolve and her lack of options, she finally relented.

Moving her into the new house lifted a big burden off my head and I felt relaxed; though that relief proved to be temporary. Soon a new and more serious issue started to raise its ugly head into our lives; which was to name to our relationship. People were unwilling to digest our togetherness as it stood in its present form. Pressure started to mount on us to either make our relationship socially acceptable or leave the area. I could not blame my neighbours for their callous attitude. They were correct on their side. Our social fabric views such relationships with suspicion and it's mostly the woman who has to bear the brunt. People get a chance to point fingers at her. Several questions are raised on her character and it is very difficult to fight everyone or answer every question. In spite of that, not yet prepared for the first choice, that of marrying each other, we went for the second option and started to search for a new home.

In no time we became aware that finding a new home was even a bigger challenge. Though a lot of houses were up for rent but none was available to us. We were amazed just how fast the words could travel. I felt a stab of disappointment piercing my insides. Frustration started to creep inside me. My mood darkened. I held up my hands in defeat.

Shobha had been watching me closely and held her responsible for my current predicament. She did not want my present to be tainted with her tumultuous past. She begged me to leave her to her own fate and move on with my life. Her suggestion was totally unacceptable to me and out rightly rejected. How could she think so little of me? I had not held her hand only to leave at the first hurdle. She tried her level best to reason her point but was unable to break my resolve. I was not going to leave her alone. I had lost her once and was in no mood to lose her again. Finally she relented to my stubbornness and we determined to face the situation together.

I went to my manager next day and finding him free, narrated my story and asked for his opinion. He appreciated my boldness and advised me to seek my parent's help.

As I had not availed any leave ever since I had joined the office, he had no difficulty in granting me a leave for one full week. Excitedly I packed my bags and left for my parental home taking Shobha along with me. It was almost evening when we reached there.

Happy to be home but hugely worried about the response from my parents, I pressed the door bell with a thumping heart, full of apprehension. Shobha felt no better and was afraid. In spite of my own nervousness, I clasped Shobha's hand, trying to give it a reassuring squeeze.

A lot of questions raced through my mind as I waited for the door to open.

How would my parents react to Shobha's presence with me?

How would they view our relationship?

Would they accept her kindly or cold shoulder her as the outside world had done to her?

Would they agree to our marriage? And if not, what could be my next course of action?

With these and many more intriguing questions plaguing

my mind I waited for the door to open.

The sound of door lock clicking open jostled me out of my thoughts and I found myself staring at my mother. We were both overjoyed to see each other after a long time. Instinctively she opened her mouth to call my father but froze mid air as her eyes fell on Shobha.

Initially she did not seem recognize her and took her for a sales girl doing door to door sales but after I had introduced Shobha to her, there were signs of immediate recognition in her eyes. She invited both of us in.

After I had freshened myself and while Shobha was in that process, I went into the kitchen where my mother was preparing tea for us. A look at her face told me that she was brimming with curiosity. Before I could open my mouth she started the conversation and came directly to the point without any prelude. Her tone was far from warm and welcoming. She inquired me about Shobha and her presence with me in a very plain and clear voice devoid of any emotions. My heart skipped several beats. The moment had finally arrived and I needed all the courage and skills to deal with it. I let out my long held breath and related all the events as they had unfolded in the best possible manner.

Unsure of what else to say, I anxiously tried to assess her mood but finding her expressionless my heart began to sink. I buried my face in her neck, as I used to do as a child when I had done something wrong and asked for her pardon. She instantly knew my intent and began to caress my hairs with her delicate fingers. A ray of hope flickered inside me. I looked at her face with anticipation but finding her expressionless once more my face sagged. I was beginning to get an idea that the road ahead was not going to be smooth. I would have to really try very hard to have my parent's permission to marry Shobha.

As usual, evening tea was served at the porch and all of us, including Shobha, took our seats around the table, joined by my father. Tea time at our house has always been a lively, fun filled hour but that day it was a totally different affair. Tense silence prevailed around the table. Everyone had so much to say but could not find the correct words do so. Shobha's unwanted presence was very much evident and as such we drank our tea in complete silence.

Once the tea was over, Shobha helped my mother clear the table and offered her hand to prepare the dinner. My mother politely declined her offer and told her to rest instead. Her passive attitude towards Shobha was proof enough that she had not yet approved her as a member of our family.

Arrangements were made for Shobha to stay in the guestroom and she retired to her room immediately after dinner. I also went to my room after spending a few minutes with my parents and took to the bed immediately but sleep eluded my eyes. However hard I might try, events of the last few days ran through my mind like a movie. Uncertain of the future, I refused to think of the worst.

As I lay in bed shifting sides, I heard footsteps of my mother going towards the guestroom. Immediately I tensed and tiptoed to the door of my room, opening a slit, I peeked out. I saw my mother enter Shobha's room. I could hear voices from inside, but they were too low. Walking tiptop I crossed over to the guestroom and put my ear to the door trying to hear the voices from inside but could not make out anything. My first instinct was to go inside unannounced but good sense prevailed and I decided against it.

Finding it useless to stand like that, I retraced my steps to my room and made to my bed again. I made a futile attempt to sleep. My ears were alert to any sound coming from outside but the only sound I could hear was the sound of clock ticking.

After almost an hour I heard my mother's steps leaving Shobha's room. My heart began to pound loudly and blood raced through my veins. I was clueless as to what transpired between the two of them. I had so many questions racing through my mind. My head was cloudy with too many issues. Did Shobha measure up to her expectations? Did my mother approve or disapprove her? What if my mother disapproved her; in which case what would happen to Shobha? Would she have to return to her old treacherous life? The mere thought of which shook me to my interiors. Next instant Shobha's gloomy, innocent face sprung before my eyes, crying inconsolably, pleading me to save her life.

Finding myself powerless to heed to her humble requests,

I hid my face in the pillow in horror. I dashed tears from my eyes and wiped my nose with the back of my hand. Muttering wordless prayers, I tried to sleep but could not do so. I passed rest of the night shifting sides or staring at the ceiling with a renewed fear of losing Shobha.

I had a trying night. Quite a number of times I left my bed and checked Shobha's door with a hope that I might be presented an opportunity to talk to her but each time I had to return empty handed. Finding myself out of luck, I resigned to my bed waited for day to break.

No sooner had the clock signaled break of dawn; I left my room and went outside. Sensing some light in the kitchen, I walked into it and saw Shobha doing some household work. A cursory glance at her was enough to let me know that she was relaxed. Seeing me enter the kitchen, she flushed a deep crimson. It did not take me something special to understand that we had leaped the most difficult hurdle. Instinctively I pulled her into my arms and hugged her tightly, hot tears of joy falling from my eyes. I was overjoyed to see that carefree girlish giggle on her face after so many days. All the pent up tension, fear and headache of the last so many days seemed to vanish in that particular moment. Feeling the warmth of my embrace, Shobha let out a most relieved smile, her own tears of joy falling freely over her dimpled cheeks.

I was eager to know what transpired between Shobha and my mother the previous night. Grabbing the first available opportunity I dragged her to my room and looked at her face excitedly; waiting for an answer to an unspoken question.

Reading my unspoken thoughts, she described in detail the conversation that went between the two ladies. My mother had gone to meet Shobha in a very agitated mood and had woken her from her sleep. Without adding any prelude she came straight to the point and wanted to know the reason Shobha wanted to marry her son.

According to my mother, I and Shobha had nothing in common and our mismatched alliance would harm our lives more than the benefits it could provide us. She even offered Shobha some financial help if she promised to move away from her son's life. But Shobha remained adamant. She was able to convince my mother that she was not after any money but truly liked her son and wanted to share the rest of her life with me.

Hurdle crossed

Shobha's unconditional love for me, her sincere affection for my parents coupled with her troubled past moved my mother's heart. In addition to being my mother she was also a woman and only a woman can understand the plight of another woman. Tears began to swell out of her eyes. Instantly she put her hand on top of Shobha's head in the form of blessing and proclaimed her to be her daughter in law.

Once the toughest hurdle had been crossed, rest of the vacations passed off happily. Sobha went about various household chores with renewed energy and confidence. She felt liberated and merry. Her carefree smile that had eluded her for the past so many years was back on her face again. She had been accepted heart and soul into our family.

Preparations for our marriage started in the right earnest and at a suitable date we tied the knot. The event was attended by a chosen few including my parents, some close relatives and Shobha's mother, who flew all the way from Canada to grace the occasion. She was shocked to hear her daughter's harrowing tale of the last few years and protested to Shobha for hiding such important happenings from her. But after coming to know that Shobha took all the pain upon herself so that her mother, who had already suffered a lot, needed some peace in her life, felt proud of her daughter's brave act and forgave her instantly. She wished her good luck for her upcoming life.

Even my manager and office colleagues came all the way to attend my marriage.

After spending few more days with my parents, courtesy my manager for granting me an extended leave, we left for my place of work. This time my mother accompanied us to help us settle down in our new life. Upon reaching our home in the colony, we got a grand reception quite in contrast to the treatment meted out to us a week back. Invitations poured in almost every day for lunch or dinner to the point that we had to turn down certain requests.

Relations between my mother and Shobha grew cordial with each passing day. Each tried to assuage the hurt feeling of the other. They soon became more like friends than the usual saas bahu. My companionship provided Shobha the much needed security and inner strength and she began to flourish. She started to regain her lost confidence. Her health began to improve and in a few days time she was back to her normal self. We made it a routine to spent most of our free time together. On weekends we went on long distance drives, hiking or picnicking. She liked to cook my favourite dishes. She was fast developing into a nice cook.

But in spite of all the good things happening to her lately, some part of her inside was not happy. I could feel a sense fear in those deep grey eyes as if she was afraid that some deep rooted evil would emerge out of her dark past to destroy her present happiness.

However hard we tried but were unable to rid her of her fears. She still loathed going into the woods. Many a times she woke up with a start during her mid sleep hour, perspiring profusely and feeling thirsty, reeling under the bout of a bad dream. Initially the instances of such bad dreams were far and few but gradually their frequency increased and with each such bout her condition worsened.

Finding myself helpless, I decided to consult a doctor and took an appointment with one. He examined Shobha thoroughly through a series of well planned sittings and came to the conclusion that she was carrying a lot of unshared burden on her mind which was affecting her mental and physical health. To get rid of that burden she would have to share it with someone and the too urgently otherwise there was a big chance that she might get into a position of no return.

Seeking to act on the doctor's advice I planned a day out one fine Sunday morning and took her on a long drive towards the jungle. Once away from the city and inside the woods I chose a convenient spot which was lonely enough to provide us enough privacy. We selected ourselves a big stone overlooking the lake and sat on it, hands locked together. She placed her head on my shoulder and closed her eyes, aiming to provide her tired mind some much needed rest.

Finding the right moment, I spoke patiently, carefully choosing my words. She glanced at me for a moment then closed her eyes again and shook her head as if it was a great effort of will, after which she crossed her arms, placed them on her folded knees and hid her face between them seeking to avoid a direct contact with my eyes. All that while I waited patiently for her to speak and that she did at last. After sitting silent for a couple of minutes, words started to pour out of her mouth.

Troubled Past

Shobha went down the memory lanes of five years back and I could feel her shudder with fear at the recollection. She had a horrific last few years.

She still remembered the day she stood first in her class. She was very happy and could not wait to break the news to her parents. On reaching her home she went dancing to her father's room with the result in her hand, expecting him to grasp her in his hands and kiss her forehead, as he always did whenever she gave him some good news. But she found his room to be empty. There was complete silence there. She could not locate him anywhere. Even her mother was nowhere to be seen. Her frantic searches yielded no results. She called out for both of them but her shouts went unanswered. An eerie feeling of something bad engulfed her mind. She went to the servant's quarters and found a lone servant. He could only inform her that her father had to be rushed to a hospital. Getting anxious, she asked one of the available drivers to take her to the hospital. As she was about to leave her house, she saw her mother entering the house, her face tense. She took Shobha inside the house. Dragging her to the privacy of her room, her mother had a very depressing story to narrate.

Her father had suffered a huge loss in his business a year

back. Every single penny had been used to repay the lenders and now he stood bankrupt. His request for a bank loan had been rejected and his relatives, who used to surround him, had deserted him. The company had been milked by too many relatives and in the time of need he had been left alone to fend for himself. With no one else to look forward to, he kept all the worries to himself or to Shobha's mother.

Tension began to show its effects on his body. His health began to show signs of deterioration. He suffered a major heart attack that day and had to be admitted to ICU ward of the hospital. He was under constant supervision. The look on her mother's face told Shobha everything. Her father's condition was not good. Shobha very much wanted to see him, but her mother advised her to wait till next morning while her mother stayed at the hospital that night.

At home, Shobha could not sleep that whole night. Her mind knew no peace. Negative thoughts continued to torment her and she found it extremely difficult to get rid of them. She expected the phone to ring anytime to give her some new on her father. She passed her time sobbing and uttering silent prayers- prayers to make her father well again.

At last the phone did ring but with it her worst fears ultimately turned real. Early next morning she received a call from her mother, her voice choked with pain and grief, informing her that her father was no more. She could clearly hear her mother crying. Shocked by the news, the phone dropped from her hand. Her body became numb. Suddenly the whole world spun before her eyes and she felt darkness everywhere. But she steadied herself immediately. She was a brave girl and could not break like that. She was the only one who had to take care of her mother.

During the next hour a hospital van dropped the body of her dead father at their house. Shobha went outside to receive the body. Her mother was alongside her dead father. Everyone gathered there was crying, except Shobha. The shock of her father's death had stirred her interiors to such an extent that she stared her father's dead body like a statue. How much did she try, she was unable to cry; tears seemed to dry up in her pretty eyes. Noticing her condition, Shobha's mother turned her attention to her and tried to console her; but she stood stone still, bereft of any feelings.

Next few hours went busy in preparing for the last rites of her father. Since she was the only child of her parents, she performed the last rites and saw her beloved father turn to ashes. Her farewell to her father was delivered in a voice which struggled to conceal its shakiness.

As days passed by, their biggest problem on how to run the house started to bother them. Most of the money was spent repaying the loans and whatever was left, was used for the treatment of her father. Her mother tried to take over the ailing business but her lack of business knowledge did more harm to it than good. People took advantage of her inexperience and plunged her into deeper troubles.

Finding some decent job also went unsuccessful. She undertook some temporary assignments but they were not enough to make the ends meet.

With no steady income and no one else to turn to, her mother decided to say it quits and return to Canada. Once the decision was made, she disposed off whatever was left of the business along with their house and any other asset that she could think off, at throwaway prices and one fine day they left the country for good and headed to Canada.

On reaching Canada, they started their life again from bits and pieces. Her mother took up a job as an office assistant in a sales company offering reasonable remuneration while Shobha enrolled herself in an evening college. During the day she picked up odd jobs to help her mother tide over the financial burden.

It was during those testing times that Shobha came into contact with an Indian family living next door to them. Their son was enrolled in the same evening school as that of Shobha. His name was Karan. He was a soft spoken boy with amiable manners. Though they had known each other only for a very short span of time, they soon turned into good friends and spent most of their spare time together. Karan's family displayed deep respects for Shobha and her mother. Within in no time the two families came very close to each other. Shobha helped the aged couple with their daily chores and looked after them whenever she could find time. Impressed by her selfless caring attitude towards others and her loving nature, they expressed their desire to accept her as their daughter in law. Shobha's mother readily consented to the idea and one fine day, the two tied the nuptial knot.

Life turned more vibrant with each passing day, presenting innumerable hopes and possibilities at every step. Shobha took good care of the house and went about her household duties with great zeal. She never let anyone feel neglected and never provided anyone any opportunity to criticize her. Her positive attitude impressed everyone.

To reciprocate her gesture, Karan's parents, showered all their love and blessings on Shobha. Not to be left behind, Karan was proving to be an excellent husband. He went extra mile to make her feel comfortable in her new role. He was very particular about meeting her various needs and never let her feel deprived. He never lost an opportunity to praise her on one pretext or other. \

Within no time Shobha became the darling of the house and soon forgot the pain of losing her father. Time started to flow by happily and in its flow Shobha washed all her tensions and worries of the last few years. She was happy and contended with her life once more.

But life cannot remain easy for long. Shobha learnt it in the days to come.

As things looked to move on smoothly, one morning Karan dropped a surprise bomb. As the family was busy taking their breakfast he expressed his desire to return to India and start a new business venture. He put his proposal before his parents and Shobha. Initially, everyone was skeptical about the proposal as it would mean starting a new life in a new land but seeing his resolve they consented to his request.

After making necessary arrangements, which took him a few months, Karan left for India, promising Shobha to take her with him once things were settled. He was given a tearful send off. Shobha felt as if a part of her own self was leaving her side. She felt depressed but hid her feelings successfully. That whole night she could not sleep but weep. Her beautiful eyes became swollen and red from the strain. The following day she went about her daily chores mechanically. While her hands worked, her thoughts roamed somewhere else. With a considerable effort she was able to perform her daily duties.

Karan reached India safely and checked into a hotel. He went about the work on his project from the very next day and soon settled into his routine. In spite of his busy schedule he made it a point to call Shobha everyday to check about her as well as that of his parent's well being. He would talk to her for hours and excitedly provide her with a daily report of his progress at his work. She could sense a feeling of loneliness in his voice. He missed her badly and his voice would turn hoarse while talking with unshed tears.

Shobha waited impatiently for his call the whole day, fighting hard to clear the lump in her throat as she answered the phone. The routine was rigorously followed for some months but as the time passed the frequency of his calls started to ebb. Soon they completely stopped.

Worried about Karan's well being, Shobha tried to contact him, but failed miserably.She tried every available means at her disposal to contact Karan but each time the outcome came out negative. Her failed efforts made her more anxious. She passed her days in great agony with no visible signs of relief. Negative thoughts began to torment her mind.

One night as lay deeply worried on her bed lost in the thoughts of Karan, her phone rang. She jumped out of her bed in anticipation and picked up the phone. She leapt with joy and relief when she heard Karan's voice on the other side. She fought a losing battle to contain her tears but did not let Karan know her condition lest it might distract him from his work.

Feeling assured of the well being of everyone at home, Karan told Shobha that he had been kept very busy with his work. His work required him to travel a lot making him miss his routine- that of calling back home every day.

Getting to know Karan's well being Shobha heaved a sigh of relief and muttered a silent prayer, thanking God for keeping her husband safe. It was during that conversation that Karan broke the good news that Shobha had heard in quite a while. He told her that he had made arrangements for both them to stay together in India and that he had sent her air tickets which she would be receiving in a couple of days.

It was the best news her ears had heard over the past so

many months. She felt overjoyed. Her dream of setting her house with Karan in India was ultimately getting fulfilled. She blushed foolishly at the thought and realized, with a shock, that it was nearly a year seen they had seen each other. All through the day she danced about the house echoing the good news. She was unable to concentrate, her thoughts turning to Karan every time she took up some work.

Rest of the day passed off uneventfully. After making arrangements for the dinner and ensuring that every member was done with it, she retired to her bed early, lost in her thoughts. She passed the whole night shifting sides, her mind busy with sweet rosy dreams.

She rose from her bed early and busied herself with the various household chores. It did not take her long to take care of her daily duties. It was the same work that she had been diligently doing everyday for last so many months with joy but that day it felt boring and cumbersome. She found it hard to concentrate on her work. Each time her mind would automatically drift towards thoughts of Karan. Her anxiousness could not escape the inquisitive gaze of her mother in law who smiled at her condition, blessing her silently for her upcoming life.

Soon the day arrived to board the flight to India. Shobha reached the airport well in time and after going through various immigration formalities boarded the plane to India with a pounding heart. She was still unable to believe that she was finally meeting Karan. Her bad luck had always come in the way of her happiness. She was gripped with a fear that something unpleasant was bound to rob her of her good fortune. Her lips continued to move in a silent prayer till the plane had actually taken off, taking Shobha with it into the waiting arms of Karan, relieving her of all her anxiety.

All through the journey she kept thinking about Karan- his heart warming smile, his caring attitude towards her, his tongue sticking out of his mouth when deep in concentration, all came before her eyes like a collage. She saw herself walking hand in hand with Karan through the rest of their lives.

The journey to India was long but her dreams were even longer. She glanced out of the window to give her tired mind a rest but her mind wandered back to Karan and a faint smile escaped her tender lips.

Her day dreaming was interrupted by the professional voice of the air hostess announcing the arrival of Delhi airport. No sooner had the plane touched the airstrip and made its way to the terminal, she sprang to her feet only to be requested by the flight attendant to remain in her seat till the plane was stationary. Unwillingly she took her seat but sprang to her feet immediately once the plane came to a halt. She could hardly wait to meet Karan. After going through all the formalities once again, Shobha collected her luggage and galloped to the exit. It was now impossible for her to remain separated from Karan. She saw him at the door anxiously watching every passing passenger, his eyes eagerly looking for her. The moment she was outside she waved frantically at him to draw his attention. Karan saw her too and came running in her direction.

Once they were close enough, she dropped her luggage, leaped towards Karan and wrapped her arms around his body, hugging him tightly. Karan was too excited to say anything. He let her hold onto him tightly, enjoying the hug. Tears of joy flowed down his cheeks. He rolled his fingers in her hairs and kissed her head passionately.

They continued to stand in that position for a while, oblivious to the amused gaze of the onlookers and when they came to their senses, they quickly separated with a big blush. Karan picked up her baggage and together they walked the distance to the parking area. Karan loaded the baggage in the parked car and settled her in the passenger seat, then moved the car out of the airport in the direction of the main city.

Driving through various city roads, they finally arrived at their residence. It was a small but beautiful house, situated in a peaceful locality. After helping her move her luggage into the house, Karan ushered her into a small, bright room. Letting her to settle in, he excused himself and left the house to attend office, promising to return early.

Shobha was feeling tired. She went to the kitchen and prepared herself a cup of coffee, carrying it with her to the living room, there she kicked off her shoes and settled herself on the bed enjoying her drink. Her tired eyes refused to remain awake any longer so she pushed the empty cup to one side of the side table, stretched on the bed and dozed off immediately only to be awoken by the arrival of Karan. She ran out barefoot to open the door and let him in. No sooner was he in; he scooped her into his arms and kissed her passionately-it was their first evening together after such a long time and both wanted to enjoy the moment. Disengaging herself from his embrace, Shobha rushed to into the kitchen, blushing deeply, to prepare evening tea for both of them. Karan followed her to the kitchen and sat beside her, watching her passionately as she prepared the tea. Once or twice when he found it impossible to control his emotions he hugged her tightly in his embrace and loved playing with the stray locks of hairs that fell on her forehead as she worked. Shobha was lost in the moment and looked forward to many more of those in her married life.

Shobha carried the tea to the porch, where they sat comfortably around a table, chatting animatedly during the hour, never letting even a moment's silence to settle between them, as if they were in a hurry to bare out all that had accumulated over the past year of their living separately. To give more time to their togetherness they decided to have dinner at the restaurant.

Time passed off happily in each other's company. Both developed a good understanding of each other. Shobha kept herself busy in the house. Her day started early. She was against the idea of hiring a maid and enjoyed looking after their house by herself. She liked cooking for Karan and took great pride in preparing his choicest dishes which she served with a lot of love at breakfast and neatly packed for lunch. After seeing him off to office she busied herself cleaning the house and putting things in order. That took much of her morning time leaving her only few minutes of rest in which to enjoy a quick cup of tea. Feeling refreshed, she went about her next task that of taking care of her personal needs. By the time she was finished it was time for lunch.

Lunch was the most relaxing time of her day. She carried her plate to the living room and ate her food on the bed, often watching television. After finishing her lunch, she felt too tired to even wash her hands and so she just slid the empty plate to one corner of the bed and stretched her tired body to rest. She was usually woken by the sound of the door bell signaling the arrival of Karan. Thereafter, it was time to perform her evening duties- preparing evening tea for them and planning the dinner. Though the same routine was followed every single day, yet she never seemed bored, on the contrary she loved her busy schedule.

Karan never let her feel alone even for a second. He phoned Shobha from office every few minutes to talk to her. He could not think of a life without her. He made his habbit to arrive from office on time so that they could spend their evenings together. He took extra care not to carry his office problems back home. During tea they chatted about general topics and the events of the day. After tea, she and Karan occasionally went for an evening walk not returning until just before dinner, which was eaten in a friendly, relaxed atmosphere. His time with Shobha was theirs only to enjoy and no one had the right to encroach upon it.

Karan loved helping Shobha with the various household chores during his free hours at home. He assisted her to prepare dinner by cutting vegetables or kneading the flour while she was busy with some other work. He was a good hand at stove himself and when the situation required, he felt no hesitation in taking over the kitchen. Whenever they invited any guests, it was his unspoken duty to share her burden of entertaining them. He never gave her any chance to complain. He had made a promise to her during their wedding to never leave her side under any situation and to keep her happy against all odds. He disliked being called a promise breaker.

On Sundays, it was his self imposed responsibility to dust the house and like a good husband he walked alongside Shobha to the market, carrying the vegetable basket. He felt no shame in doing so; instead it gave him immense pleasure. Their spare time was spent working out things for their new home or going out on a drive where they could spend their time away from the city life.

Both took great pleasure in testing each other's patience. Many a times Karan alarmed Shobha with his childish prank when she was deeply engrossed in her work and least expecting it. She when felt irritated and retaliated, it led to more such pranks. Not a single day passed when they were not involved in a heated argument over some trivial matter prompting them to stop talking to each others for hours. But things would settle down soon and they would be laughing together again.

As she thought her life was moving smoothly, Karan shocked her once again. All of a sudden he started to show signs of change. Innumerable times he arrived late from his office, sometimes heavily drunk. Not in control of his senses, he would shout and abuse Shobha on one pretext or the other. Unable to fathom the reason behind that sudden change she tried to reason with him but failed miserably in her attempts. On the contrary, Karan became more violent. They fought regularly. It became a routine for him to skip dinner and retire to his bed early. They talked less and less with each other. On many occasions she cried herself to sleep. In the mornings, when she confronted Karan, he would just nod his head innocently as if nothing ever happened and would leave for office early. She felt so lonely and hurt. How much Shobha might try she was unable to pick the reason behind that sudden change. Whenever she questioned Karan about his changed behavior, he shrugged her off rudely. Tension started to creep between them. It was the first time that she doubted her relations with Karan.

Then one fine evening everything became crystal clear on its own.

With the intention of providing some rest to her tired mind and body Shobha stretched herself on a couch and closed her eyes. Within no time she was fast asleep only to be awoken by the sharp sound of the door bell. Half asleep, she looked at her watch. It was six in the evening. She got off the couch and ran to open the door. Karan was standing outside holding the hand of a beautiful lady. Shobha was stunned in her tracks. Without greeting her or looking back at her, Karan entered the house with the guest leaving behind a speechless Shobha at the door.

She had many questions racing through her mind. She closed the door impatiently and headed to where Karan and the guest were seated. Once inside she looked at Karan inquiringly. As an answer to all her questions, Karan introduced the lady as his new wife. Stunned into silence, Shobha could not believe what she had just heard. Thinking that she might have heard it wrong, she requested him to repeat what he had just said and getting the same answer left her speechless. There was darkness before her eyes. All her dreams of spending a beautiful life with Karan came crashing down on her head. Fate had played a cruel joke with her life again. Unable to bear the pain she left Karan and headed for her bedroom, crying hysterically and bolted the door to her room. That night also she cried herself to sleep.

When she came out of her room, it was light outside and rays of the morning Sun filled the house. Karan and the lady were nowhere to be seen. She searched the house frantically but could not locate either of them; instead she found a letter in Karan's hand writing, the contents of which shook Shobha to her insides.

According to letter, the name of lady in question was Rimmi. She was the daughter of a wealthy industrialist who had partnered with Karan in his new project. Rimmi's father had invested heavily in Karan's company without which the project would have not seen the light of the day. If Karan's business was his life then Rimmi's money that was its lifeline. Needless to say, Rimmi's father owned Karan and burdened him under the debt of his gratitude.

Karan's frequent visits to Rimmi's house turned them into good friends and soon their friendship developed into a special liking for each other. Karan was so enamoured of her mesmerizing qualities that he started to follow her like an obedient slave. She loved to play with his emotions while he kept his eyes closed to the reality.

Rimmi's father never objected to their relationship. Instead, he fanned their emotions even more. They started to spend more and more of their time together. Finally one day, Rimmi told Karan to leave Shobha and come to her forever. Not bold enough to take his own stand and considering his future prospects, Karan consented to leave Shobha and marry Rimmi. After the marriage, Karan was supposed to move into a palatial new house with Rimmi where he planned to spend the rest of his life. He had left Shobha the divorce papers, which she was expected to sign and move out of his life.
Placed in the envelope along with the letter were the divorce papers.

With trembling hands Shobha smoothed the creased papers and went through its contents. Earth shook beneath her feet when she read the contents of the papers. Frivolous charges were levelled against her to seek divorce. She could not believe what she had just read.

Shobha felt cheated by Karan but her biggest failure was her lack of judgment about him. Here was a man she thought she knew more than herself but that myth lay cruelly broken before her very eyes.

She saw her heart lay shattered before her in thousand pieces.

Searing pain surged through her insides, a pain of being let down by someone so close to her heart. She found it difficult to decide whether to laugh or be angry at those allegations.

In a state of dilemma, she picked up the phone and called Karan, who immediately responded to her line. Her first instinct was to protest his wrong doing but her wounded pride prevented her from doing so. Her self esteem discouraged her from assuming the role of being his half a wife only while his true allegiance lay somewhere else. It must be all or nothing. She wanted to own him completely.

Encouraged by her resolve, she just congratulated Karan, wished him good luck for his future life and hung up. She signed the divorce papers and left the house for good never thinking once as to where her decision will lead her to. Suddenly her life had turned so murky that she was not sure of anything anymore.

With nowhere else to go she contacted her only close childhood friend and apprised her of the situation. Her friend took no time to think and immediately offered her a stay at her house till she was good enough to take care of herself on her own.

As a result of that goodwill gesture, Shobha was able to find a roof over her head while a little help from her friend's husband secured her a reasonably well paying job.

She was full of gratitude towards her friend and her husband. She thanked them from the core of her heart and once she was well enough financially, she moved into her own apartment.

New pain

Shobha began to settle in life her again and started to overcome her pain of losing Karan when one day she received a call from her friend's husband. After exchanging pleasantries, he bluntly came to the reason for giving her a call. He requested for a lone evening with her at his outhouse to reciprocate his goodwill gesture. Sensing his intentions but to be sure, she asked him to be more specific and when he requested her to spend a night with him at his outhouse, without mincing his words, she was stunned. She could not believe what she had just heard. She had held that man in high esteem and there he was who left no stone unturned to shatter her belief. Anger flared in her insides and she turned him down rudely.

Not expecting a cold response he banged the phone off, warning her of dire consequences in case she did not accede his request. He threatened to defame her name publicly. She thought about the conversation the whole day and into the night and arrived at a decision. She would have to leave the town for good if she was to preserve her relations with her friend and save her married life. She packed her bags and left for the railway station with no destination in particular.

It was quite late in the night and the station bore an empty look except her. With no train was expected to arrive soon, she took a bench, thinking about her future plans. She only had a small amount of money on her with no one to call to for help.

As she sat on the bench with her mind drifted towards the problem at hand, she heard the sound of approaching footsteps from behind her and before she could react, two strong hands closed her mouth with two more hands lifting her from her seat and bundling her into a waiting car.

No sooner was she pushed inside, the doors were closed shut and the car sped its way into an unknown direction. She was made to stay in that position for about an hour before she could hear the engine slowing down. As the car came to a halt, its doors were pushed open and she was pulled outside.

Once up on her feet, she saw herself facing a lonely house. A couple of strong looking men escorted her into the house and locked her in a room. The room where she was held hostage was cold and dark without any arrangements for sunlight. The only opening in the room was a solitary door which was locked from outside. She tried hard to draw attention by banging at the door vigourously but no one seemed to come to her rescue.

When she got tired in her attempts to free herself, she sat down in a corner and started to cry at her piteous condition. After a while she heard the sound of door clicking open and saw a man holding a tray of food which he gave her and turned back to leave. Shobha caught the sleeve of the retreating man and inquired in a terrified voice as to where she was and why was she taken hostage. The man remained silent, shrugged off her hand and left a crying Shobha behind.

Though Shobha had not eaten anything for quite some time yet she did not feel hungry. Terror had eaten up all her appetite. She pushed the tray to one side and moved to a corner of the room. The same exercise continued throughout the day, a man would enter the room, drop a tray of food and leave without uttering a single word. Trays of food piled up but she did not touch even a single one of them. She passed her time sobbing and uttering silent prayers.

When the door opened the next time she saw a different man. On close inspection the face seemed familiar and when recognition dawned upon her she was stunned. It was her friend's husband on the door, smiling a wicked smile. Things started to get clear. She had been kidnapped by her friend's husband. He entered the room and sat besides Shobha. He forcefully took her chin in his hand and forced her head up so that she was facing him. His intentions were very clear and his eyes were shinning with lust. He tried to persuade Shobha to accede to his requests but when she did not budge he became violent. He drew out a cane from his jacket and thrashed her with it mercilessly, hurling abuses at her. Her heart rendering cries echoed throughout the building, searing pain started to engulf her entire body. But all her cries of pain fell on deaf ears and no one came to her rescue. He continued with his gory act till she was able to take it no more and fell unconscious. Feeling frustrated her friend's husband left the room with a strict warning of inflicting even more pain next time if she did not relent.

After he had left, Shobha hid her face in her hands and cried loudly at her pitiable condition caressing her swollen body. Pain was starting to become unbearable and so was her hunger; yet she preferred to die than to take a bite of food. So the next morning when her friend's husband came to her, she was left with not much energy to fend for herself and resist his advances. She resigned to her fate muttering silent prayers in the hope of some divine intervention.

And the divine intervention did occur. When her friend's husband was about to succeed in his evil intentions she heard sharp cries outside. Sound of running footsteps echoed through the hallway followed by sound of gunshots. Next instant the door to her room swung open and in came the inspector holding a smoking gun. In one swift action, he grabbed my friend's husband roughly and dragged him outside where all his aides had already been taken into custody.

After regaining her composure and taking care of her disheveled appearance, Shobha came out of the room to find that the gang had already been bundled into a waiting police vehicle and whisked away. The inspector requested Shobha to come to the police station with him and file a formal complaint against her friend's husband.

On reaching the police station she was both overjoyed and relieved to see Ajit, her office colleague, sitting in the inspector's cabin. It was Ajit who had tipped the police about the possible kidnapping when Shobha did not turn up at the office for three full days. The inspector alerted his team and a search through the area led to Shobha's rescue.

Once the formalities were over and Shobha was free to go, she thanked the inspector and Ajit and stood up to leave. It was quite late in the night. Ajit offered her to drop her at her apartment.

That night turned out to be the most difficult nights of her life. The moment she tried to close her eyes to sleep, the events of the last few days came running before her eyes like a movie. Horrific images of her friend's husband, his wicked smile and his attempts to outrage her modest made her perspire profusely. She began to tremble in her bed and the hairs on back of her arms stiffened. She was startled by the slightest noise outside, which continued to torment her for days to come. She would wake up from her sleep with a start, perspiring immensely. Her eyes would turn blank from fear and she would spend the rest of the night wide awake. Her condition deteriorated with each passing day and would have continued to worsen had it not been for Ajit. He spent days after days taking care of Shobha, often risking his own health. As a result of his humane act and with the passage of time her condition began to improve and in a few weeks time she was back to normal.

Shobha resumed her office soon and settled down in her official duties with the help of Ajit. Though the last few days had been full of bad memories, there had been one positive outcome. She had found a dependable friend, Ajit, who could be relied upon during difficult times.

They developed a liking for each other. Ajit took good care of her. He visited her regularly and they enjoyed the evenings together. He worked hard to make sure, with fair amount success, that the blisters of her past memories got cured and did not leave their mark on her future life.

Sharing most of their time together brought Shobha and Ajit closer. Soon they opened their hearts to each other. Shobha had never felt so happy in her entire life. She started to weave colourful dreams for her upcoming life once again. She pictured herself clutched firmly into the arms of Ajit, staring lovingly in his beautiful eyes, saying absolutely nothing, as if words were frozen in her mouth.

After a month long courtship, they finally decided to marry. It was during one of their usual evenings at a restaurant while they were enjoying coffee that Ajit proposed her. Though she had expected it coming, yet it came to her at a time when she was least expecting it, giving it a touch of drama. She was stunned momentarily. When she came to her senses after a few minutes, she was overjoyed. She felt excited to imagine herself being addressed as Mrs. Ajit. Everything felt like the part of a fairy tale. Her happiness knew no bounds. The very thought of sharing their lives together created ripples of excitement in her heart. All her worries and hardships were soon going to be over. She would have someone on whose shoulder she could lean her head on in times of need and who would understand her feelings.

Their marriage was scheduled for the coming month. Being short on time she got busy with her arrangements with renewed vigour. She planned to invite all her office colleagues at the wedding ceremony, as they were her only family in India. Her mother had not been keeping well lately and was unable to travel long distances, moreover she did not want her know about her past travails. She planned to take Ajit with her after their marriage to Canada to meet her mother and seek her blessings. Ajit helped Shobha with the preparations and often spent time in her apartment planning the occasion.

Deceit and Escape

Ajit came to Shobha's apartment to dicuss some last moment preparations. It was evening and time for tea so Shobha went into the kitchen to prepare tea for both of them. As she was preparing the tea, she chanced upon a conversation between Ajit and some unknown person on the other side of the phone. What strained her ears was the mention of her name. Thinking that Ajit was inviting a friend of his for their wedding she took it casually. But what struck her was the tone of the conversation; it was too low to be casual. It was as if Ajit was talking to someone surreptitiously. She tiptoed to where Ajit was standing and hid behind a door, trying to make out the conversation. What she heard shook the earth from beneath her feet when reality dawned upon her. She could not believe what she had just heard. Ajit was a human trafficker, who entrapped innocent, young girls in his emotional bond and forced them into flesh trade. He had used the same trick on Shobha as he had done with so many other girls. He had plans to sell her to a rich businessman for a hefty amount. He had started to work on his plans from the very first day he had set his sight on Shobha. She perfectly met his client's needs.

All of Shobha's dreams came crashing down to the floor. Her heart had been shattered once again. Life soon turned from pleasant to unpleasant. Ajit had put her in an invidious situation. Fear and pain of being betrayed by her senses yet again, surged through her entire body.

She wanted to cry out loudly but that was not the right time for that. Her immediate concern was to get as far away from Ajit as possible without raising his suspicion. Her mind started to work frantically. She would have to leave her bags behind as packing them would raise suspicion. She would have to run empty handed. Time was running out for her and she had to make her move immediately if she was to save her life. She had no doubt in her mind that Ajit would not let her escape easily. He would chase her like a hound to hell. The best chance for her was to get as far away as possible from him in the shortest possible time before he realizes the escape.

On the pretext of getting some sugar from the market she took her purse, put all her savings in it whatever she could lay her hands on, and left the house. Once outside she hired a cab and made her way to the railway station. All through the ride she glanced back nervously to check if Ajit had noticed her absence. Her fears turned real when she saw Ajit following her cab. Immediately her muscles tensed and she requested the driver to pick up the speed. When that did not help to shake off Ajit from her pursuit, she requested the driver to roam about the roads aimlessly for some distance instead of moving directly to the railway station. Her pallid appearance did not go unnoticed but instead of asking any questions, at that crucial time, the driver did as was requested without a single word of protest. That that step too could not deter Ajit from following Shobha and so proved futile.

Fearing his passenger to be in deep trouble, the cab driver could not hold on to his curiosity any further and asked her the reason about her strange behaviour. Taking him as her only possible chance, she told the driver everything. The cab driver seemed a nice man. He advised Shobha to jump off the cab at the right moment as he slowed the vehicle down and hide herself inside a laden truck which was standing idly alongside the road. In the meantime he would try to shake Ajit off her trail. Once that was done, he would come back and take Shobha to the railway station.

Accepting his plan, Shobha went for the truck at the first available opportunity and made her way to its back where a lot of cartons were loaded. The cab scampered into a lane keenly followed by Ajit. Heaving a sigh of temporary relief, Shobha pulled a carton and placed it under her head to rest her tired body while she waited for the cab to return. Before she knew it, she had dozed off.

She did not have an idea about how long she had been asleep but when she awoke she was still travelling though the road had turned bumpy. She peered through the load and found that the truck was moving through some hills. The sight of unknown terrain made her panic. Her first reaction was to raise an alarm and stop the truck but then she quickly changed her mind. Her ultimate aim was to get as far away from Ajit as possible and she had so far succeeded in it, so why spoil her chances. Thinking about it, she resigned herself to her fate and lay down again.

After moving for few more hours, the truck finally came to a halt in front of a dhaba and the driver went inside. Sensing her chance, she jumped off the truck. After disguising herself, as best as she could, with whatever resources she had at her disposal she went inside the dhabha and ordered herself a hefty lunch. She felt famished as she had not eaten anything for quite a long time. She devoured her food in no time.

She was so engrossed in having her food that she did not notice the driver leave the place and finally when she did notice the driver's absence, she hurried outside only to find that the truck was already gone. She limped to the ground in disgust. It was now pointless to cry over the spilled milk so she soon regained her senses and started to count her options. Her tight situation gave her the insight to view each option very carefully. She chose one mentally, which she thought was best under the given circumstances and stood up with resolution.

She went inside the dhaba and settled her bill. As night was about to fall she walked up to the village and inquired about some place to rest for the night. She had no difficulty in finding one at a very cheap price. Though the dwelling was well below her comforts she had no choice but to accept it.

She spent the next few days in that hut, moving out rarely, causing a strain on her savings and her funds started to run out. She was in urgent need of fresh money. To overcome her monetary crisis she decided to walk to the nearby town and look for some work.

With some efforts she was able to find work as a domestic help. Though she felt uncomfortable initially doing that work, within no time she began to enjoy it. The experience encouraged her to take few more such jobs. Soon she began to undertake odd jobs which were available aplenty in the area; providing her both financial as well as personal security. Her appearance got adapted to the colours of the local life and she became one of the local people.

Her work required her to go to the town for which she had to walk through the jungle. Every day she would saunter through the jungle, admiring the natural beauty as she passed by, talking to the birds in a language which only she and they could understand. She liked spending time in the jungle.

At last peace and happiness

It was during one such errand that Shobha saw a seeming familiar figure sitting beneath a tree lost in his thoughts that raised her curiosity. Years of separation had blurred my image in her memory and without doubt she was unable to recognize me immediately. How hard she might try she was unable to place the face she just saw. With confusion clouding her thoughts she walked past the jungle, resolving to look for that face again. She reached the spot early the next day and hid behind a tree, keeping an eye on me.

It was then that I had seen her peering at me and as I walked towards her, she got frightened and sped away. But that did not deter her to know more about me. When I came looking for her in the jungle, she was watching me from a distance but could not muster the courage to come out in the open. She had mistaken me to be one of the cohorts of Ajit; so she requested the villagers not to reveal her real identity to me. She followed me surreptitiously.

With persistent efforts she was able to muster enough information that convinced her as to who I was and once her mind was clear of all the doubts, her heart yearned to meet me. She started to look for a favourable opportunity when she could catch me alone. She did not have to wait long. It was presented to her when I was about to leave the restaurant after the party and that's how she came into contact with me again. The subsequent events were already in my knowledge. I had finally succeeded in finding the missing links to her ordeal.

After narrating her story she stopped and went silent for a few minutes expecting me to say something. But when I did not respond even after a long time and maintained my silence, she pulled her head away from her folded hands, glanced up and searched my face for a reaction; a scared expression dotting her beautiful face.

She feared that once I come to know of her troubled past I would leave her and she would be left alone to fend for herself as she had been doing for the past so many years.

It was necessary for me to reassure her. Her capacity to suffer had exceeded its limits. Though it was not the right moment, yet her queer expression made me laugh and I squeezed her into a tight embrace, letting her know that I would never leave her side come what may.

That simple gesture was enough to make her feel assured. Shobha felt relaxed as if a heavy burden had been lifted of her head. She leaned her head on my shoulder and cried passionately.

She was finally able to bid adieu to her painful memories which she had been her companion of the last so many years.

Her frazzled heart had finally been healed....

www.ingramcontent.com/pod-product-compliance
Lightning Source LLC
LaVergne TN
LVHW050419160726

843469LV00041B/1141